M IS FOR MICHIGAN

Alphabet Book For Kids

This Book Belongs To

....

A is for Apple Blossom

Michigan's state flower

B is for Black-eyed Susan

A common wildflower in Michigan

Michigan is known for its cherry production

C is for Cherry

D is for Detroit

A major city and historical place in Michiga

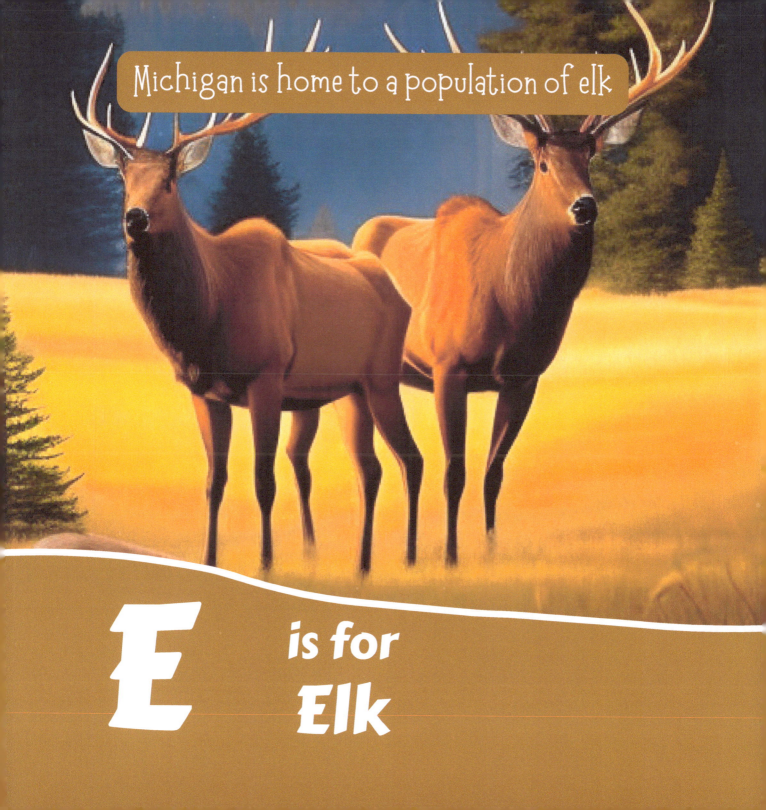

F is for Ford Museum

A famous historical place in Dearborn, Michigan

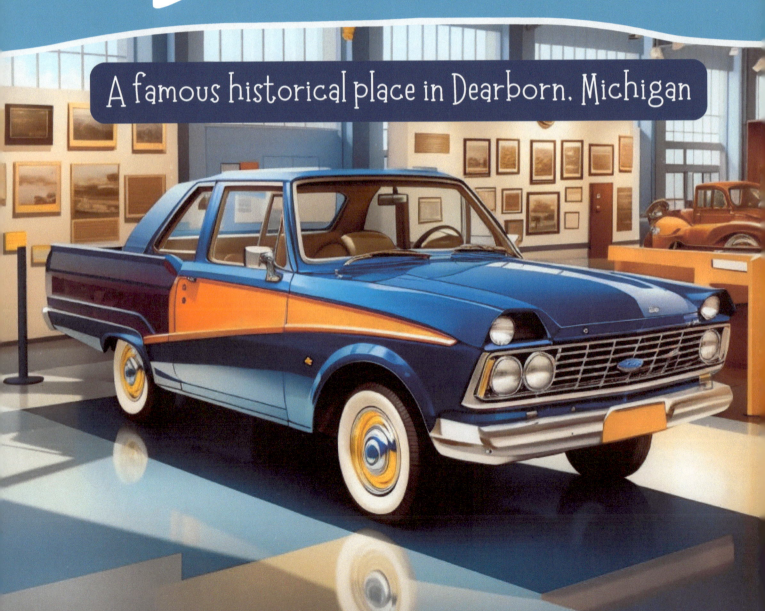

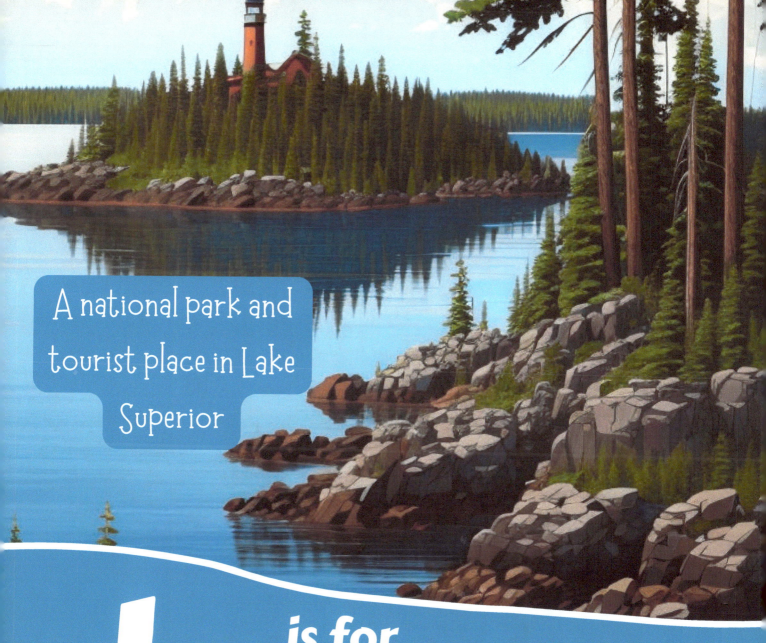

A national park and tourist place in Lake Superior

I is for Isle Royale

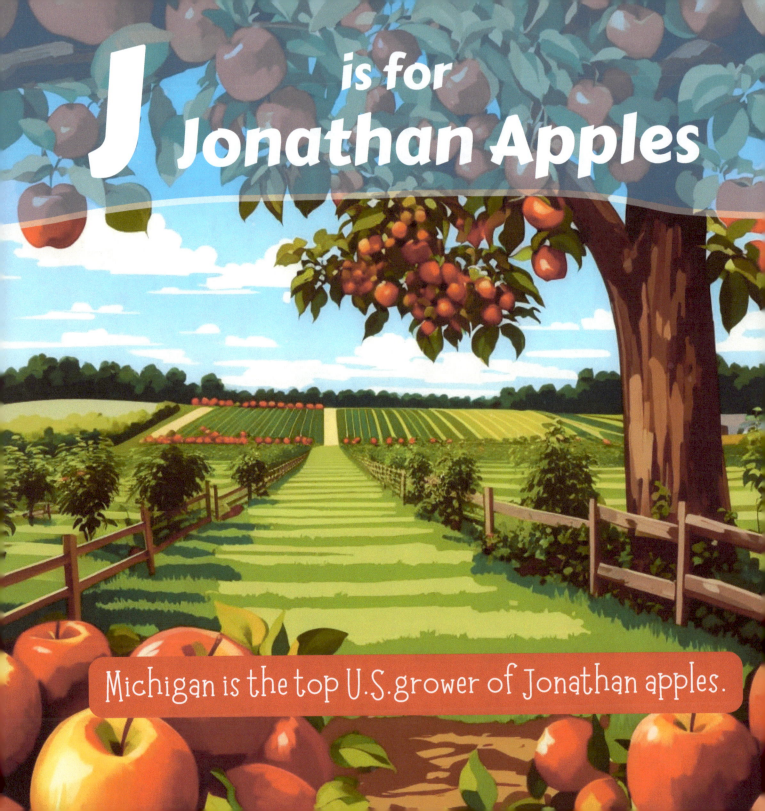

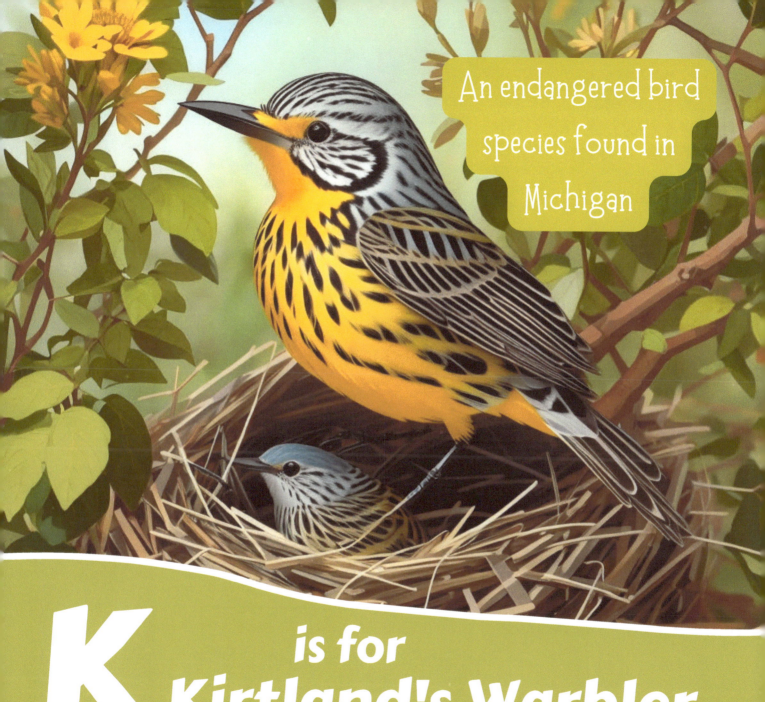

An endangered bird species found in Michigan

K is for Kirtland's Warbler

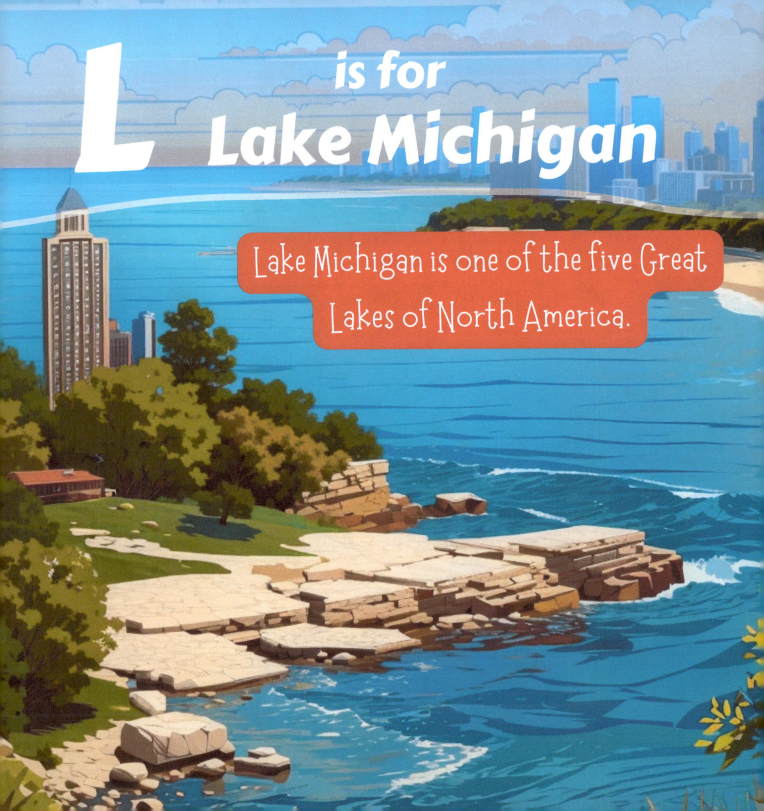

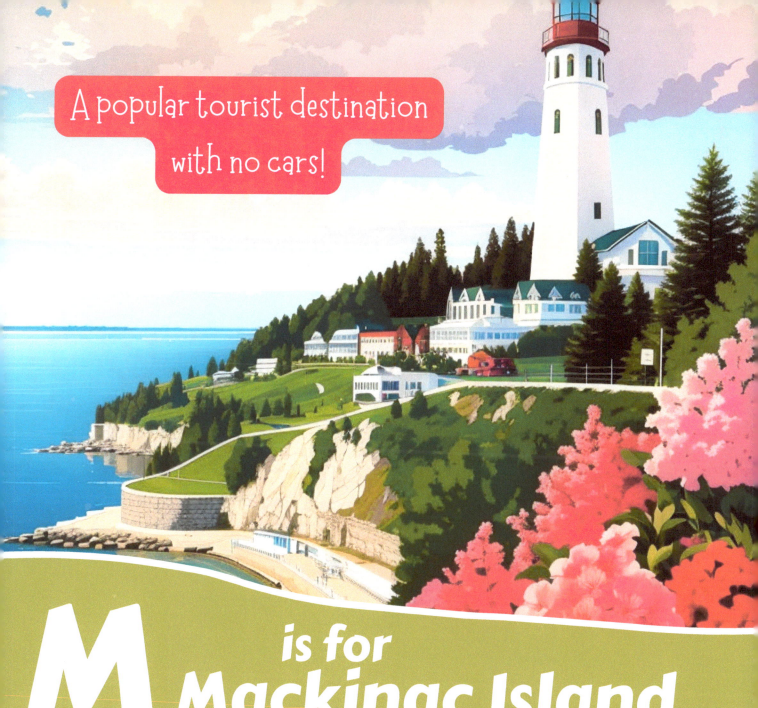

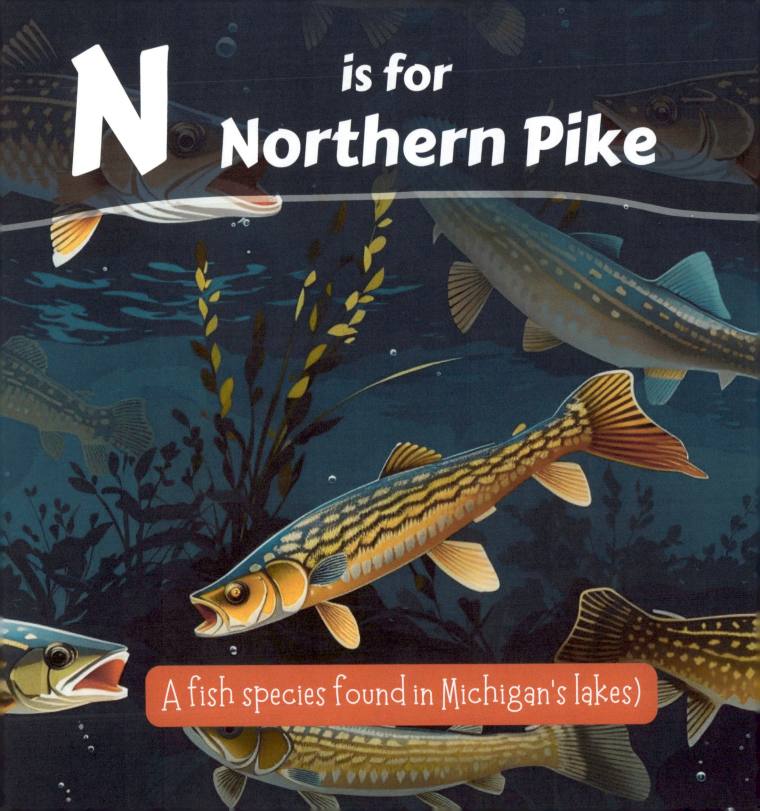

N is for Northern Pike

A fish species found in Michigan's lakes)

P is for Painted Turtle

Official state reptile of Michigan

A type of tree found in Michigan

Q is for Quaking Aspen

R is for Robin

American Robin, a common bird species in Michigan

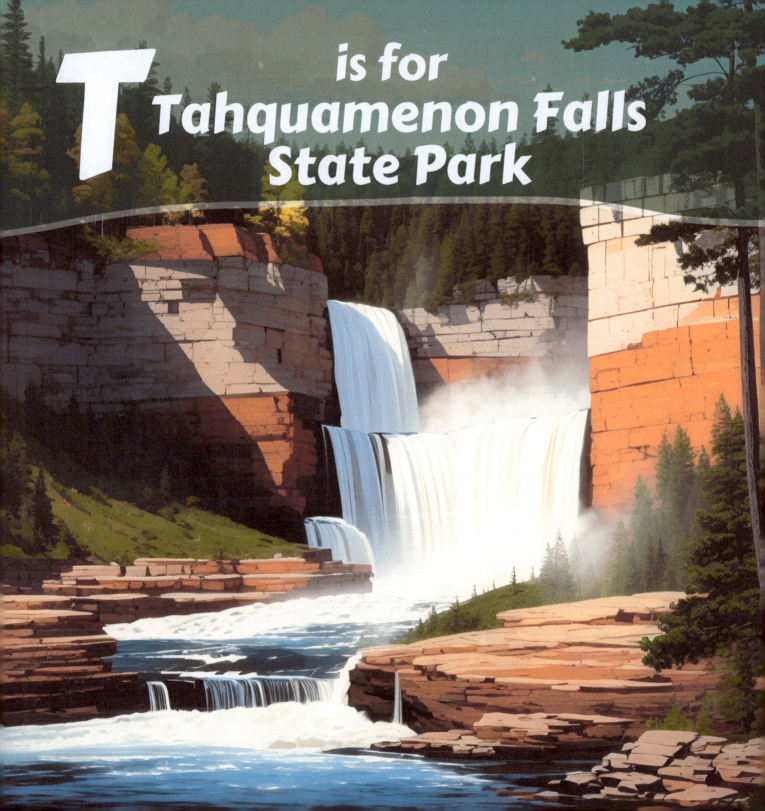

A region in Michigan with unique natural beauty

U is for Upper Peninsula

V is for Greenfield Village

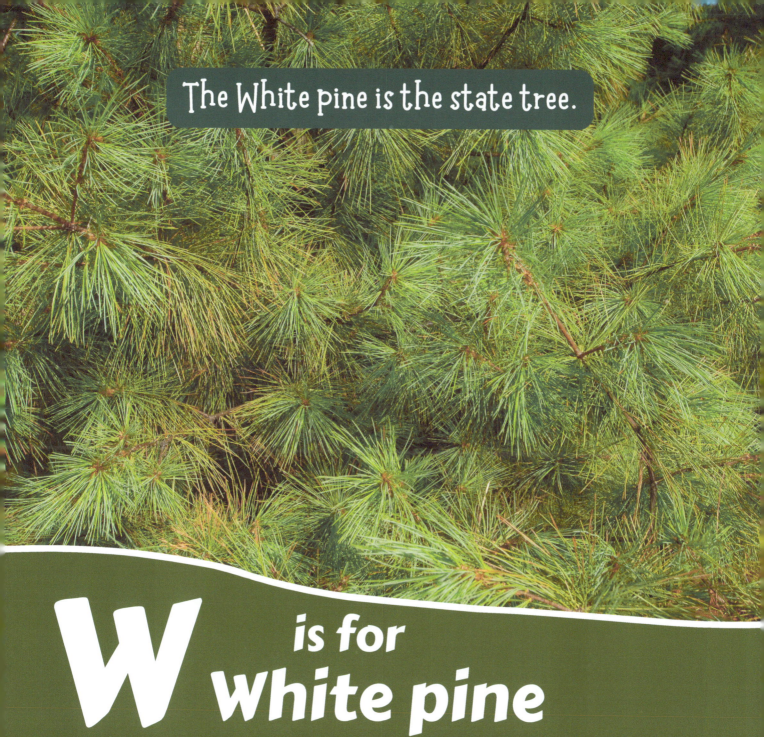

The White pine is the state tree.

W is for White pine

X is for Xerophyte

A type of plant adapted to Michigan's dry regions

Yearly snowfalls average between 40 to 70 inches a year

Y is for Yearly snowfalls